Nelson Spelling

Pupil Book 3

OXFORD

UNIVERSITY PRESS

Book 3 Scope and Sequence

Unit	Pupil Book Focus	Pupil Book Extra	Pupil Book Extension	Resource Book Focus	Resource Book Extension
1	sp, spr finding target words	wordsearch puzzle	adding vowel letters in the correct place within given sentences	word building	identifying synonyms; using a dictionary to write definitions
2	all, al using the al prefix	using al suffixes	identifying prefix meanings	word building	using l/ll; adding the ly suffix
3	soft c finding target words	matching ice words with definitions	identifying ce, ci, cy patterns	identifying ice/ace patterns	alphabetical ordering
4	silent letters b and k finding target words	completing a table with b + ing/ed	doubling last letter before suffix	sorting silent letters	using silent letters
5	le, el, al, il endings finding target words	completing a table with le + ing/ed	nnel pattern quiz	completing endings puzzle	cloze activity; writing definitions
6	some y endings cloze activity	doubling last letter before y ending	dropping e before suffix	word building	making and writing adjectives
7	making plurals making simple plurals	making es plurals	changing y to i plurals	identifying and using s/es	using ies/ys
8	y+er, y+est finding target words	making comparatives	making superlatives	word building	using y+er/y+est
9	ing, ed selecting target words	adding ing/ed	dropping e before suffix	adding ing; writing sentences	doubling final letter and dropping the e
10	soft g, ge, dge sorting by word family	dropping e before suffix	making nge words and definitions	word building; writing funny sentences	matching definitions; writing sentences
11	wa, qua finding target words	target word quiz	making singular possessive sentences	finding target words; completing wordsearch	solving quiz with clues
12	tion, ation finding target words	cloze activity	identifying shion/tion; making tion family words	adding tion to build words	using ation/ition/otion in sentences
13	sion finding target words	identifying sion rhyming words	matching words to definitions	adding sion to build words	using ession/ission/ossion in sentences
14	adding suffixes applying suffixes	changing y to i before suffix	making word families	adding ness/ment; making sentences	identifying syllables
15	contractions deconstructing contractions	identifying when to use you're / your	making contractions	deconstructing and making contractions	making contractions; writing sentences

The darker cells introduce statutory material for this year group in the National Curriculum for England.
The paler cells denote revision of a topic covered in previous years.

Unit	Pupil Book Focus	Pupil Book Extra	Pupil Book Extension	Resource Book Focus	Resource Book Extension
16	**homophones** finding target words	choosing homophones	identifying and writing mnemonics	word-matching; writing sentences	cloze activity; using target words in sentences
17	**silent letters o, h, and c** finding target words	finding *ch* words in wordsearch	using a dictionary to find definitions	identifying letter patterns	identifying silent letters; correcting spelling test
18	**ei, y and other tricky words** finding target words	target word quiz	identifying homophones	identifying *le* letter patterns; writing sentences	target letter quiz; writing definitions; rhyming clues
19	**ous** cloze activity	matching adjectives with nouns	identifying *ious/eous* words	building *ous* words	identifying letter patterns; writing sentences with target words
20	**dis, mis, in, im, il, ir** finding target words	understanding prefix meanings	using a dictionary to find related words	target letter patterns; picture clues	completing wordsearch; writing sentences
21	**un, de, re, pre, non** finding target words	understanding prefix meanings	using a dictionary to find related words	building words using target prefixes	completing wordsearch; writing sentences
22	**ly ending** finding target words	adding *ly* to root words	changing *y* to *i* before suffix	word building	writing sentences with target words; identifying *ly* words
23	**sure, ture** finding target words	target word quiz	identifying *ture/cher* words	word building	identifying letter patterns; writing sentences
24	**wh, ph** cloze activity	finding small words within words	target word quiz	word building	cloze activity; *wh* words quiz
25	**compound words** making compound words from word sums	making compound words	identifying compound words	building compound words	making compound words; using target words in sentences
26	**silent w** finding target words	making word webs	completing wordsearch	word building; writing sentences	cloze activity; correcting incorrect spelling in prose
27	**words in words** finding small words within short words	finding small words within longer words	identifying small words as spelling support	finding words within words	finding words within longer words; using a dictionary to find words containing three small words
28	**dictionary work** vowels and consonants	alphabetical ordering	finding and writing dictionary definitions	alphabetical ordering	putting homophones in alphabetical order

sp
spr

The flowers are **spr**outing.
Spring has **spr**ung!

Key Words

spin ✓
spot ✓
spill
spark
speak
spike
spout
special
specific
spell

spray
sprout
sprint
spring

especially

Focus

Copy the key words neatly into your book.
Tick the ones you can find in the picture.

Extra

A Lots of the key words beginning with **sp** and **spr** are hidden in this puzzle. Some go across and some go down.
Write them in your book.

s	p	e	a	k	s	s	p	r	i	n	g
p	x	q	e	s	p	i	l	l	o	u	x
i	m	p	s	p	r	o	u	t	a	z	r
n	l	e	s	p	a	r	k	f	t	o	p
s	p	e	l	l	y	s	p	r	i	n	t

How many did you find?
6 = good
8 or more = brilliant!

B Write three sentences.
In each sentence include at least one of the words you have found in the puzzle.

Extension

The vowel letters have been left out of these sentences.
Copy the sentences neatly, putting the vowels back.

1 Th_ c_t j_mp_d _v_r th_ f_x.

2 H_ g_t cr_ss _nd r_n _ft_r th_ c_t.

3 Th_ c_t r_n _p th_ tr__.

4 "Y_u w_ll h_v_ t_ c_m_ d_wn
 _n_ d_y," s__d th_ f_x.

Remember, the vowel letters are **a, e, i, o** and **u**.

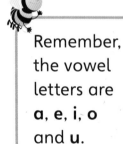

We **al**ways love the sm**all** animals.

Key Words

fall
tall
small
stall

also
always
already
almost
although
altogether

usual
capital
sandal
pedal
signal
hospital
occasional
special
accidental

Focus

Remember, a prefix is a letter or letters added at the beginning of a word.

When we use **all** at the beginning of a word, we always drop one **l**.

all + most = **al**most

A Make a new word with each of these words by adding the **al** prefix.

1 most	**2** ready	**3** together
4 so	**5** mighty	**6** though

B Write a sentence that includes at least three **al** words.

Many words that end in **al** are adjectives that are made from other words.

bride (noun)   brid**al** (adjective)

Remember, **adjectives** describe nouns.

A For each of these nouns write the related adjective by adding the **al** suffix.
Check your answers in a dictionary.

1 norm	2 topic	3 centre	4 music
5 nature	6 accident	7 comic	8 mechanic

B For each of these adjectives, write the related noun.

1 occasional   2 signal   3 original   4 factual   5 historical

Extension

Prefixes have meanings.

al	means **all**	**al**ways
ad	means **towards**	**ad**vance
a	means **on** or **in**	**a**board

All right is always two words!

A Copy these words and write what you think it means next to each one.
Use the prefix to help you.

Use a dictionary to help you.

1 admire	2 almighty	3 asleep
4 adjoin	5 altogether	6 aground

B Write a list of at least three words with each of these prefixes. Use a dictionary to help you.

a   ad   al

Tricky Words
though
although

soft c

I like mice
They're so nice
I'll tell you twice
That I like mice!

Key Words

city
centre
cell
cellar
cereal
circus
certain
cycle

ace
race
face

recent
concert
December

except
excellent

Focus

A Copy the list of key words neatly in your book. Tick all those that you can see in the picture.

B Write the key words that have both a **soft c** and a **hard c** in your book. Try to think of two more words like this.

When the **c** sounds like **s** we say that it is 'soft'. When it sounds like **k** we say it is 'hard'.

office   dice   rice   police   price   twice   notice   spice

Match an **ice** word from the box with each clue.
The first one is done to help you.

1 room used
  for business   *office*

2 tastes good with curry

3 Throw a six!

4 flavouring for food

5 two times

6 they chase criminals

7 gives information

8 can be cheap, can be
  expensive

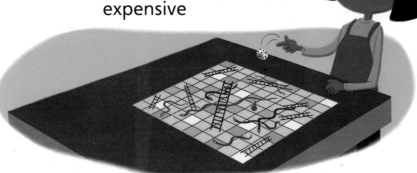

Extension

A Sort the words in the box into the correct list.

cymbal   accident   centre   recent   cygnet
Cyprus   certain   cyclist   mice   bicycle
century notice   cylinder   cyber   special
celery   exercise   decide   cinder   circle

> In words
> that have
> a **ce**, **ci** or
> **cy** letter
> pattern the
> **c** is usually
> '**soft**', like **s**.

ce words	**ci** words	**cy** words
celery	cinder	cylinder

B Now try to add more words to your lists where the
ce, **ci** or **cy** letter pattern isn't at the beginning of
the word, like **except**, **pencil** and **juicy**.

silent letters b and k

lamb
knock
climb
knife
thumb
comb
crumb

Key Words

lamb
comb
climb
crumb
thumb

knee
kneel
knew
knife
knit
knot
knock

Focus

A Look at these picture clues.
Write the key words in your book.

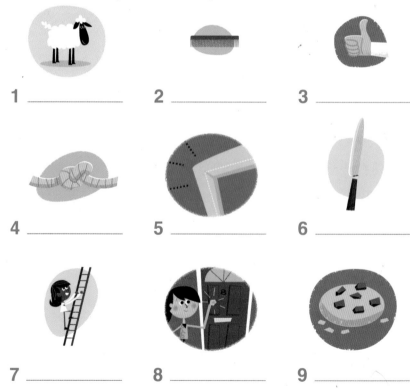

1 _____ 2 _____ 3 _____

4 _____ 5 _____ 6 _____

7 _____ 8 _____ 9 _____

B Underline the letters you do not hear or say when you read the words.

C Write two other silent **b** or **k** words.

Extra

Adding suffixes to silent **b** words is easy, like this:

comb   comb**ing**   comb**ed**

Remember,
a **suffix** is
an ending.

Copy and finish this chart.

comb	combing	combed
lamb		
climb		
thumb		
plumb		

Extension

Adding a suffix to silent **k** words can be difficult.
Sometimes we must double the last letter before adding
ing, **ed** or **er.**

knit   knit**t**ing

Tip! Look at the letter before the last letter.
Is it a single vowel (**a, e, i, o,** or **u**)?

knit	yes	knitting
knock	no, **c** is not a vowel	knocking

Be careful!
Kneel has
two vowels
before the
last letter.

A Copy and finish this chart.

knit	knitting		
knock		knocked	knocker
knot			
kneel			

B Write a fun sentence that has at least four
silent letter **k** words.

Tricky
Words
know
knowledge

le, el, al, il endings

Double, double, toil
and trouble:
Fire burn and
cauldron bubble.

William Shakespeare
(*Macbeth*)

Key Words

candle
handle
bottle
paddle

angle
bangle
rectangle

camel
cancel
gravel
novel

sandal
metal
signal
hospital

fossil
nostril
tonsil

Focus

Copy the key words neatly into your book.
Tick the ones you can see in the picture.

Extra

We add **ed** to a verb if the action has happened in the **past**, and we add **ing** if it is happening at the **present** time.

Copy the table then add **ing** and **ed** to each verb.
The first one is done to help you.
Remember what happens if the verb ends with **e**.

Remember, a **verb** is a doing or being word.

verb	present	past
grumble	grumbling	grumbled
tumble		
crumble		
fumble		
jingle		
scramble		

Extension

All the answers to these clues end with the letter pattern **nnel**.
The first one is done to help you.

1 This is a narrow stretch of sea, as between England and France.   channel

2 You might use this when you wash.

3 This is a dog's house that you can keep in the garden.

4 This is a passage for roads or railways through mountains.

5 You use this to help you pour liquid into a bottle.

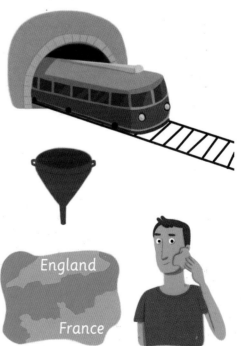

England

France

some y endings

stormy

windy

grumpy

cheeky

chilly

dirty

Key Words

chilly
frilly
windy
happy
frosty
dusty
lucky
rainy
sleepy
cheeky
stormy
dirty
grumpy

Focus

A Look at the picture. Copy and finish each sentence with a key word.

1 It was a r_____ day.

2 I was feeling g_____.

3 Jenny was smiling and looking h_____.

4 "It is l_____ I planted the seeds yesterday," she said.

B Find a key word to rhyme with:

1 snappy   **2** lumpy   **3** mucky

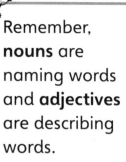

Extra

Nouns can be made into adjectives by adding **y**, like this:

rain   a rain**y** day

But remember, if the letter before the last is a single vowel (**a e i o u**), double the last letter, like this:

m**u**d   m**uddy** clothes

Remember, **nouns** are naming words and **adjectives** are describing words.

A Copy these nouns and add **y** to make them into adjectives.

1 flash   **2** wind   **3** rock   **4** luck   **5** rust
6 fog   **7** sun   **8** fun   **9** spot   **10** sleep

B Write three sentences, each using at least one of the words you have made.

Extension

To make an adjective with a **y** from a word ending in **e**, remember to drop the **e**, like this:

slim~~e~~ + y = slim**y**

Copy and complete this chart.

noun	adjective
wave	wavy
laze	
bone	
	rosy
smoke	
	stony

making plurals

Key Words

cats
dogs
ducks
frogs
cows
chickens

foxes
ostriches

monkeys
donkeys

ponies
flies
butterflies

wolves
calves

Focus

When we talk about only **one** thing it is **singular**.

When we talk about **two or more** things they are **plural**.

We usually add **s** to show that we mean more than one.

singular	plural
cat	+ **s** = cat**s**
tiger	+ **s** = tiger**s**

Write the plural of these words.

1 cat	**2** dog	**3** duck	**4** frog
5 cow	**6** chicken	**7** badger	**8** swan
9 snail	**10** worm	**11** snake	**12** rabbit

Extra

If a noun ends with **s**, **x**, **ch** or **sh**, we add **es** to make it plural.

singular	plural
peach	+**es** = peach**es**

A Copy this table. Make the plurals of these nouns.

singular	ostrich	fox	box	bus	branch	latch	brush
plural							

B Add **s** or **es** to each of these words to make them plural.

1 bush   2 car   3 class   4 street   5 box

6 fox   7 torch   8 match   9 pass   10 passenger

Extension

To make a noun that ends with **y** plural, change the **y** to **i** before adding **es**.

But if the letter before the **y** is a vowel (**a e i o u**), just add **s**.

singular	plural
fly	fl**ies**
monkey	monke**ys**

> **Tricky Words**
> potato
> potatoes

Copy this table. Make the plurals of these nouns.

singular	fly	turkey	pony	baby	donkey	butterfly
plural						

Sometimes, to make a noun plural we use a different word or we don't add anything!
Write the plurals for these nouns.

1 man   2 mouse   3 sheep   4 woman   5 child

y + er
y + est

mudd**y**   muddi**er**   muddi**est**

Key Words

windy
windier
windiest

foggy
foggier
foggiest

sunny
sunnier
sunniest

rainy
rainier
rainiest

Focus

A Look at these weather pictures.
Write the key words in your book.

1 _____   2 _____

3 _____   4 _____

B Copy all the key words into your book that have double letters.

If we want to turn an adjective that ends in **y** into a special adjective to compare **two** things, we change the **y** to **i** and add **er**, like this:

My friend is funny.   She is funn**ier** than me.

Remember, an **adjective** is a describing word.

Copy these sentences and fill in the gaps by making a comparative adjective from the word in bold. The first is done to help you.

1 **windy**   It is <u>windier</u> today than it was yesterday.
2 **chilly**   I am feeling a lot _____ than I was at home.
3 **stormy**   It was _____ last night than it was on Friday.
4 **cloudy**   It is _____ now than it was this morning.

Extension

If we want to turn an adjective that ends in **y** into a special adjective to compare **more than two** things, we change the **y** to **i** and add **est**, like this:

My friend is funny.   She is the funn**iest** person I know.

A Copy and complete this chart.

pretty	prettiest
smelly	
moody	
gloomy	
	cheekiest
sleepy	
	messiest

B Write sentences using three of the **est** words you have made.

ing
ed

wash**ing**   wash**ed**

Key Words

cooking
cooked
washing
marrying

hugging
hugged
shopping
dragging

waving
waved
smiling
skating

Focus

A Choose a verb ending in **ing** from the key words to match each picture.

1    2    3

4    5    6

7    8    9

B Write about what happens to **shop**, **hug** and **drag** when **ing** is added.

Extra

Remember, when you add **ing** or **ed** to a short word, look at the letter before the last letter.

If it is a **consonant**, or **two vowels** together just add **ing**.

If it is a **single vowel**, double the last letter and add **ing** or **ed**.

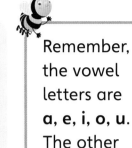

Remember, the vowel letters are **a, e, i, o, u**. The other letters are consonants.

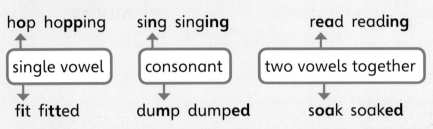

hop hop**p**ing   sing sing**ing**   rea**d** read**ing**

single vowel   consonant   two vowels together

fit fit**t**ed   dum**p** dump**ed**   soa**k** soak**ed**

For words ending in **w**, **x** or **y**, <u>don't</u> double the last letter.

play   play**ing**   play**ed**

Add **ing** and **ed** to each of these verbs.

1 clap	**2** tug	**3** nod
4 slip	**5** strap	**6** stoop
7 screw	**8** munch	**9** saw
10 bang	**11** fill	**12** relax

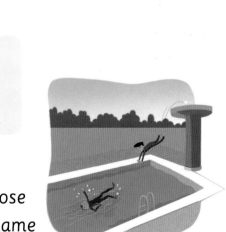

Extension

Remember, to add **ing** or **ed** to a word that ends with **e**, we normally remove the **e** first.

sha**ve**   sha**ving**   sha**ved**

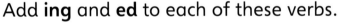

A Add **ing** and **ed** to each of these verbs.

1 chase	**2** dive	**3** poke	**4** close
5 strike	**6** tune	**7** save	**8** blame
9 choke	**10** rule	**11** behave	**12** skate

B Write three more verbs that end in **e** and add **ing** and **ed**.

soft g, ge, dge

The billy goats had to do**dge** the hu**ge** wolf to cross the bri**dge**.

Key Words

edge
ledge

bridge
fridge
ridge

dodge
lodge
lodger

fudge
judge

cage
page
wage

damage
garage

Focus

A Sort the key words and any other words that you can find in this picture into these families. Write them in your book.

adge   edge   idge   odge   udge

B Write a word ending with **ge** that means:

1 bigger, beginning with **l**
2 very big, beginning with **h**
3 where cars are kept, beginning with **g**
4 a small house in the country, beginning with **c**.

When we add **ing** to words ending with **ge,** we must first drop the **e.**

Like this: lodge + **ing** = lodg**ing**

A Add **ing** to each of these words.

1 dodge	2 hedge	3 nudge	4 judge
5 plunge	6 range	7 sponge	8 bulge

B Write a sentence about the Focus picture opposite, using at least one of these **ing** words.

Extension

strange   range   fringe   plunge   orange   hinge   sponge

All the words in the box have the **nge** letter pattern. In the table below some of the words are missing and some of the definitions are missing. Use the words in the box to help you finish the definitions.

A **definition** is a meaning of a word.

fringe	hair cut straight across the forehead
range	
	metal joint on which a door swings
sponge	
	a dive
strange	
	a juicy fruit

wa
qua

Key Words

was
wasp
wash
want
wander
water
watch
wallet

swan
swap
swamp

war
ward
warn
warm

towards
afterwards

quantity
quality
squash

Focus

A Find the **wa** words in the picture. Write them in your book.

B Draw a picture of something that begins with **swa**. Write its name.

Extra

Write a key word from the Key Words box to answer these riddles.

1 a big white bird that rhymes with **gone**

2 not very hot and rhymes with **storm**

3 makes you clean and rhymes with **cosh**

4 to exchange something and rhymes with **mop**

5 to walk slowly, that rhymes with **ponder**

Extension

A Write the following in a shorter way. The first one is done to help you.

> To show something belongs to someone, we add **'s**, like this:
>
> Wanda**'s** bone
>
> The bone belongs to Wanda.

1 the wings belonging to the wasp   *the wasp's wings*

2 the watch belonging to Megan

3 the wallet belonging to the man

4 the water belonging to the fish

5 the swamp belonging to the hippo

B Write a list with the names of five friends and one thing that belongs to each one, like this:

Aimee's dog called Barney

' is called an **apostrophe**.

tion
ation

Birthday Instruc**tion**s
1 Turn in the direc**tion** of the toy sta**tion**.
2 Open your toy box a frac**tion**.
3 Find your present!
4 Enjoy your birthday celebr**ation**s.

Key Words

station
nation
relation
education
operation
vaccination
multiplication

position
competition

eruption
description

mention
attention
invention

Focus

A Match a key word to each of these pictures.

1 _____   2 _____   3 _____

4 _____   5 _____   6 _____

7 _____   8 _____   9 _____

2+5=
4+3=
2+9=

B Copy all the key words that end with **ation** into your book.
Write a sentence using at least two of these words.

explanation   operation   population
examination   station

Copy and complete these sentences using words from the box.

1 My sister went to hospital for an o_____.

2 We have our school maths e_____ today!

3 China is the country with the biggest p_____.

4 We met our Nan at the s_____.

5 My teacher wanted an e_____ for why I hadn't finished my work.

Extension

The **shun** sound at the end of a word is nearly always spelt **tion**.

Never spell it with **sh** except in **fashion** and **cushion**.

Write a **tion** word in the same family as each of these words.
The first one is done to help you.

You might find a dictionary helpful.

1 celebrate   celebration

2 operate   3 create   4 calculate   5 situate

6 evaporate   7 locate   8 investigate   9 educate

sion

I must do my revi**sion** for my test on divi**sion**. I must practise comprehen**sion** so no more televi**sion**!

Key Words

vision
television
revision
division

invasion
occasion

version
diversion
excursion

pension
extension

explosion
erosion

Focus

A Match a key word to each of these pictures. Write the answers in your book.

        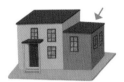

1 _____ 2 _____ 3 _____

4 _____ 5 _____ 6 _____

7 _____ 8 _____ 9 _____

B Write sentences about two of the pictures.

Extra

A Find two words that rhyme with each of these words.
Write them in your book.

    1 version   **2** television   **3** pension

B Write a short passage no longer than three sentences. Each sentence must include at least one of the key words.

Extension

Read the words in the box and the list of definitions.
Match each word to its definition. The first one is done for you.

> Remember, a **definition** is the meaning of a word.

discussion   permission   admission
comprehension   expansion   expression

1 talking something over   discussion

2 understanding

3 getting larger

4 letting people enter

5 a way of saying something

6 freedom to do something

Tricky Words
occasion   occasionally
possess   possession

adding suffixes

Key Words

helpful
hopeful
wonderful
careful

careless
homeless
pointless
hopeless

pavement
payment
treatment
enjoyment
improvement

illness
darkness
laziness
silliness

Focus

A Add **ful**, **less**, **ment** or **ness** to finish these words. Write the words in your book.

1 wonder _____

2 pay _____

3 dark _____

4 care _____

B Look at these words.

point   base   entertain   excite   judge
improve   fear   sense   end   use

You can add **less** to some and you can add **ment** to others.
Make two lists, one for each type.

Remember, to add a suffix to a word that ends in **y**, where the **y** sounds like **ee** in b**ee**, change the **y** to **i** and add the suffix, like this:

happ**y** + **n**ess = happiness
beaut**y** + ful = beautiful

> A group of letters added to the end of a word is called a **suffix**.

Add **ness** or **ment** to each of these words and then use four of the new words in sentences.

1 lazy	2 naughty	3 nasty	4 empty
5 enjoy	6 pay	7 happy	8 heavy
9 dry	10 pretty	11 silly	12 employ

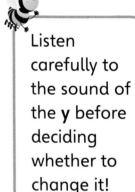

> Listen carefully to the sound of the **y** before deciding whether to change it!

Extension

Adding different suffixes to a word can change its meaning. Use the suffixes in the box to make as many new words as you can using the words below.
The first one is done to help you.

ly   ful   less   er   able   ed   ing

1 help   helpless   helpful   helping
          helped   helper   helpfully

2 wish   3 care   4 fear

5 pain   6 friend   7 walk

Wishing Well

Check-up 1

Focus

What are these? The first letters will give you a clue.
Write them in your book.

1 sp_____ 2 b_____ 3 c_____ 4 c_____

5 l_____ 6 k_____ 7 c_____ 8 c_____

9 c_____ 10 f_____ 11 m_____ 12 h_____

13 w_____ 14 s_____ 15 s_____ 16 t_____

Extension

A Copy these nouns and add **y** to make them into adjectives.

1 wind   2 luck   3 sun
4 fog   5 wave   6 smoke

B Write the plural of these words.

1 cow   2 chicken   3 badger   4 swan
5 box   6 class   7 torch   8 brush
9 pony   10 baby   11 monkey   12 donkey

C Add **er** and **est** to each of these nouns to make adjectives.

1 warm   2 cloudy   3 foggy   4 misty

D Add **ful**, **less**, **ment** or **ness** to finish these words.

1 excite   2 sense   3 wonder   4 dark

E Add **ness** to each of these words.

1 lazy   2 happy   3 silly   4 naughty

contractions

It's too late.
United **can't** make it!

Key Words

I'll
he's
she's
there's
it's

where's
here's

don't
isn't
doesn't
didn't

won't
can't

couldn't
wouldn't
shouldn't
hasn't

Focus

Write the two words that have been joined to make these words.
The first is done to help you.

1 don't   do not

2 I've   **3** he's   **4** she's   **5** I'll

6 don't   **7** can't   **8** won't   **9** doesn't

10 wouldn't **11** weren't **12** shouldn't **13** where's

Read these sentences quietly to yourself.
Try putting **you are** or **your** in the gaps. Which one makes sense?
Copy the sentences into your book, choosing **you're** (which means '**you are**') or **your** to finish them.

1 Can I come to _____ party?

2 No, _____ too young!

3 I think _____ being unkind.

4 _____ wrong!

5 But _____ dad said I am old enough!

Extension

A Make contractions from these pairs of words.

   1 should not   2 could not   3 would not

   4 you would   5 you will   6 you have

B Use each contraction in **A** in a sentence.

> Remember, a contraction is one word made from two e.g. did not = **didn't**.

homophones

Key Words

rain
rein
reign

dear
deer

knight
night

not
knot

flour
flower

sun
son

berry
bury

ball
bawl

Ratty and Mole **rowed** down the river in the **tale** 'The Wind in the Willows' by Kenneth Grahame.

Focus

Look at these picture clues.
Write the correct word in your book.

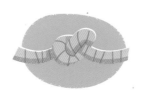  

1 _____   2 _____   3 _____

4 _____   5 _____   6 _____

7 _____   8 _____

Extra

Homophones are words that sound the same, but which are spelt differently and have different meanings.

We passed **two beech** trees as we walked **to** the **beach** to **see** the **sea**.

Remember, **homo** means 'same' and **phone** means 'sound'.

A Write a homophone for each of these words.

1 whether	2 who's	3 scene	4 mist	5 plane
6 fair	7 great	8 grown	9 hear	10 meet

B Write sentences about a trip to the beach using four of the pairs of homophones in **A**.

Extension

Mnemonics (pronounced *nemonics*) are short phrases or rhymes that help us remember things. We can use mnemonics to help us to remember which homophone to use.

hear or here? We h**ear** with our **ear**. It's **here** not **there**.

A Copy these words and phrases. Underline the letters in each that the mnemonic helps us to remember.

1 beech or beach   The beach is by the sea.
2 heard or herd   I heard with my ear.
3 steel or steal   Dad tried to steal Mum's cup of tea.
4 meet or meat   We can eat meat.

B Make up your own mnemonics to help you remember how to use these homophones correctly.

1 serial or cereal   2 stair or stare
3 hair or hare   4 board or bored

silent letters o, h and c

Two y**o**ung puppies are d**o**uble the tr**o**uble!

Focus

A Match a key word to each of these picture clues. Write the answers in your book.

1 _____ 2 _____ 3 _____

4 _____ 5 _____ 6 _____

B Write a sentence about one of these pictures.

Extra

Many words we use in English have originally come from other languages.

Words with **ch**, when the **h** is silent, are usually from the **Greek** language.

echo   chrome   chronic

Make a list of words with a silent **h** that you can find in this puzzle.
You should be able to find eight.

v	i	c	x	a	q	f	e	c
g	c	h	r	o	n	i	c	h
k	k	r	e	y	h	g	h	o
i	t	o	q	k	x	p	o	r
q	b	m	c	h	o	i	r	u
c	h	e	m	i	s	t	f	s
c	h	a	r	a	c	t	e	r
o	s	c	h	e	m	e	b	n

Extension

A Use a dictionary to find the definition of these words.

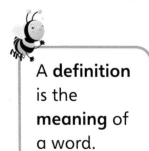

A **definition** is the **meaning** of a word.

1 chronic   2 scheme   3 echo

4 character   5 chemical   6 mechanic

B Write a sentence using one of the words in **A**.

ei, y and other tricky words

Eight chefs visit the **pyramids** in **Egypt**.

Key Words

vein
reins
weight
freight
sleigh
neighbour
eight
eighth
height
they
obey
Egypt
pyramid
natural
quarter
woman
women
length
caught
surprise
strength

Focus

A Match a key word to each of these picture clues. Write the answers in your book.

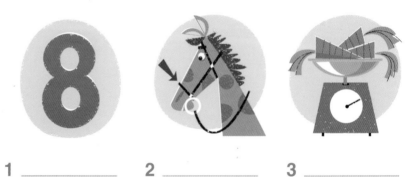

1 _____   2 _____   3 _____

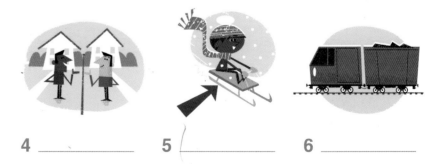

4 _____   5 _____   6 _____

B Write a homophone for each of these words.

1 vane   2 rain   3 eight   4 slay

Who am I?
Write the answers in your book.

1 I'm the opposite of disobey.
2 I'm one more than seven.
3 I'm a whole divided into four.
4 I'm the distance from one end to the other.
5 I'm the plural of woman.
6 I'm unexpected.
7 I'm where pharaohs were buried.
8 I'm what the cricketer did to the ball.

Extension

A Copy these words in your book.
Write a homophone next to each word.
The first one is done to help you.

> Remember, a **homophone** is a word that sounds the same.

   1 wait *weight*   **2** slay   **3** vain   **4** rain

B Use your dictionary to help you write a definition for each of these words.

   1 reign   **2** sleigh   **3** weight   **4** vein

ous

enormous

nervous

Key Words

dangerous
enormous
famous
generous
jealous
nervous

curious
furious
previous
serious
various
victorious

hideous
courteous

Focus

Copy these sentences into your book. Fill the gaps with words from the key word list.

1 The London Eye is f_____.

2 It is an e_____ big wheel.

3 I felt n_____ about going on it.

4 Dad said it isn't d_____.

5 My friends will be very j_____ when they know I've had a ride!

Extra

A Match these adjectives with their nouns.
Write them in pairs in your book.

> Remember, **adjectives** describe nouns.

nouns	adjectives
danger	suspicious
jealousy	victorious
victory	nervous
nerve	disastrous
disaster	jealous
suspicion	dangerous

B Add at least another two pairs to your list.

Extension

A In the box are some of the more tricky words ending in **ious** and **eous**.

curious   hideous   vicious   conscious   outrageous
precious   delicious   gorgeous   spontaneous

Copy the words into your book.
Sort them into two lists, like this:

ious words   **eous words**

curious   hideous

B Add more words to your lists.
What do you notice about the **eous** list?

dis mis
in im
il ir

impossible

misbehave

Focus

A Match a key word to each of these pictures. Write the answers in your book.

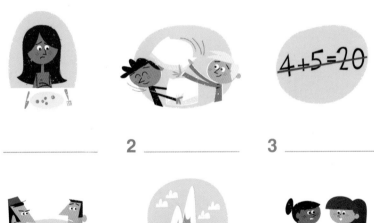

1 _____   2 _____   3 _____

4 _____   5 _____   6 _____

B Write sentences using at least two of these words.

Remember, a **prefix** is a group of letters at the beginning of a word that changes its meaning.

Some prefixes give a word the opposite meaning.

obey   **dis**obey   possible   **im**possible

A Copy these words and underline the prefixes.

1 dislike   2 misspell   3 incorrect

4 illegal   5 immature   6 irregular

7 disappear   8 inactive   9 misprint

When we add a **prefix**, don't worry if it doubles some letters. Just add it!

B Add a prefix to these words to make them have the opposite meaning.

1 agree   2 visible

3 mature   4 behave

5 responsible   6 patient

7 legible   8 relevant

Extension

Use a dictionary to help you write three other words beginning with each of the six prefixes **dis**, **mis**, **in**, **im**, **il** and **ir**.

The first one is done to help you.

1 dis   distrust disintegrate dislocate

un de re pre non

unhappy

untie

untidy

Key Words

unhappy
untidy
untie
unwell
unfold
undress

decode
defrost
defuse

refill
revisit

preset
preview

non-stop
non-starter
nonsense

Focus

A Add **un** to make the opposites of these words.
The pictures will help you.
Write the answers in your book.

1 _____ dress   2 _____ well   3 _____ fold

4 _____ happy   5 _____ tidy   6 _____ tie

B Write a sentence about one of these pictures.

Remember, a **prefix** is a group of letters at the beginning of a word that changes its meaning.

Some prefixes give a word the opposite meaning.

equal **un**equal   sense **non**sense

Here are some other important prefixes.

mist **de**mist build **re**build set **pre**set

Prefix has a <u>pre</u>fix!

A Copy these words and underline the prefixes.

1 unpopular   2 depress   3 revisit   4 prejudge
5 unzip   6 decode   7 replay   8 prehistoric
9 unsure   10 prepaid   11 defuse   12 non-stick

B Add the prefix **re** to these words to make them have the sense of redoing something.

1 build   2 play
3 visit   4 pay
5 write   6 place
7 form   8 fill

A Use a dictionary to help you write three other words beginning with each of the prefixes **de**, **un**, **re**, **pre** and **non**.
The first one is done to help you.

1 de   decay   destroy   deface

B Write a sentence to explain what each prefix means.

Tricky
Words
describe
description

ly ending

I go to school dai**ly**.
I go swimming week**ly**.
I go on holiday year**ly**.

Focus

A Match a key word to each of these pictures.
Write the answers in your book.

1 _____ 2 _____ 3 _____

4 _____ 5 _____ 6 _____

B Write sentences using at least two of
these words.

The **ly** suffix starts with a consonant letter so it is simply added straight on to most root words, like this:

    sad   sad**ly**   cross   cross**ly**

If the root word ends with **l** we still add **ly**, like this:

    usual   usual**ly**

Add **ly** to each of these words.

1 bad

2 steep

3 nice

4 slow

5 glad

6 helpful

7 like

8 silent

9 original

10 eventual

Extension

When adding **ly** to words that end with **y**, we change the **y** to **i** before adding **ly**, like this:

    happy   happ**ily**

A   Add **ly** to each of these words.

    1 merry   2 cheery   3 heavy

    4 pretty   5 angry   6 happy

B   Write sentences using at least three of the **ly** words you have made.

sure
ture

A scary crea**ture**
was guarding
the trea**sure**.

Focus

A Match a key word to each of these pictures.
Write the answers in your book.

1 _____ 2 _____ 3 _____

4 _____ 5 _____ 6 _____

B Write sentences using at least two of
these words.

A Choose a word from the box to match each clue.
Write the answers in your book.

> future   mixture   pleasure   creature
> treasure   fracture   puncture   sculpture

What am I?
1 I'm several different things put together.
2 I'm a box of valuable items.
3 I happen if you fall badly.
4 I'm the opposite of the past.
5 I am what a sculptor makes.
6 I'm a hole in your bike tyre.
7 I'm a small animal.
8 I'm another word for happiness.

B Make up a similar 'What am I?' puzzle using
other **ure** words for your friends.

Extension

> Most words with the 'tcher' sound at the end are spelt **ture**.
>
> na**ture**   pic**ture**
>
> But when the root word ends in **ch** we just add **er**, like this:
>
> tea**ch**   teach**er**

A   teacher   sketcher   catcher   stretcher
      richer   snatcher   pincher   muncher

Copy the **cher** words in the box into your book.
Neatly underline the **ch** in each one.

B Write a sentence using at least two of the words.

wh
ph

Where is the **wh**ale?
Where is the dol**ph**in?

Key Words

when
where
why
which
while
white

what
who
whose
whole

pheasant
phrase
photo

alphabet
elephant
dolphin
nephew
trophy

Focus

Copy these questions.
Choose **wh** key words to fill the gaps.

1 _____ are we going?

2 _____ will the bus come?

3 _____ bus are we catching?

4 _____ isn't Kamil coming with us?

How many small words can you find in these **wh** and **ph** words?
For example, **where**: he (w**he**re); her (w**her**e);
here (w**here**).

1 wheel   2 white   3 wheat
4 when   5 whisper   6 whiskers
7 earphone   8 pharmacist 9 photograph

Extension

elephant   dolphin   photograph   autograph
saxophone   telephone   atmosphere   microphone

What am I?

Write the answer from the box in your book.

1 I'm the largest land animal.
2 I'm a signature.
3 I can make sounds louder.
4 I'm the air around the Earth.
5 I'm used to talk to people far away.
6 I swim in the sea.
7 I'm a musical instrument.
8 I'm an image of people, places or things.

compound words

playground

playtime

Focus

Copy and finish these word sums.
Write the answers in your book.

1 paint + brush =

2 earth + worm =

3 foot + ball =

4 egg + cup =

5 goal + keeper =

6 tool + box =

Write as many compound words as you can that have the following as part of the words.

1 body   2 thing   3 eye   4 no

5 day   6 time   7 green   8 foot

9 way   10 grand   11 path   12 post

> Remember, when two words are joined, the new word is called a **compound word**.

Extension

A Find and copy the compound words in this postcard into your book.

Dear Grandmother,

We are having fun here at the seaside, making sandcastles and playing football. At lunchtime we walked up the footpath from the beach and had strawberry ice cream at the cafe on the clifftop.

From your loving grandson,
Carl

Mrs Greensmith
Windmill House
Woodland Road
Southend
SD43 5SN

B Write some compound words that you might find at the supermarket.

silent
w

wriggle

sword

wreck

Key Words

wrap
wreck
write
wrinkle
wrist
wrong

wrath
wren
wrestle
wriggle
wring

whole
answer
sword

Focus

A Write the key words that match each picture in your book.

1 _____   2 _____   3 _____

4 _____   5 _____   6 _____

 $3+4=5$

7 _____   8 _____   9 _____

B Underline the silent letter in the words you have written.

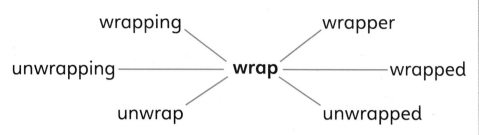

This **word web** contains some of the words you can make by combining the root word **wrap** with prefixes and suffixes.

> Remember, a **prefix** is added at the beginning of a word and a **suffix** is added at the end of a word.

A Make a word web for each of these root words below. Write them in your book. They might not have as many related words as **wrap**.

> write wriggle wrong wrestle

B Write the root word hidden in these words.

1 wholesome 2 wrecking 3 wrinkly

4 wrongfully 5 unanswerable 6 wringer

Extension

Ten words with silent letters are hidden in this puzzle. Write the answers in your book.

q	r	h	y	m	e	s	i	g	n
b	c	o	m	b	c	l	i	m	b
e	w	u	e	r	t	k	n	o	w
m	y	r	e	i	g	n	i	o	k
a	u	t	u	m	n	e	q	n	n
r	h	i	n	o	c	e	r	o	s

1 I'm 60 minutes.

2 I'm found in poems.

3 I'm when a king or queen rules a country.

4 I'm a leg joint.

5 I'm an animal with a large horn.

6 I'm what you do when you write your name on a card.

7 I'm the homophone of 'no'.

8 I'm used to keep hair tidy.

9 I'm a season.

10 I'm what children like to do in trees.

words in words

me

in

something

thin

met

Key Words

that
them
then

want
what
where
when

your
because
another
something
someone
friend
therefore

Focus

Spelling is often easier if you can find smaller words within longer words.
Copy these words and neatly underline a small word hidden in each one.
The first one is done to help you.

1 be<u>cause</u>   2 what   3 friend   4 your
5 when   6 that   7 them   8 want
9 where   10 whim   11 then   12 another

Write all the smaller words you can find in each of these words.
The first one is done for you.

1 carefully   careful care car a are ref full fully
2 another   3 someone   4 grandmother
5 clockwise   6 unfortunately   7 forgetful
8 unsatisfactory 9 knowledge   10 therefore

Extension

A Write your full name. Can you find any smaller
words in it?

B Find a word with five smaller words within it.
Write the word and the smaller words.
Use a dictionary to help you.

C Make word pictures to remind you how to spell
these words. The first one is done to help you.

1 want   w<u>ant</u>

2 glove   3 string
4 shook   5 share
6 battery   7 office

dictionary work

dictionary *n.* a book of words in alphabetical order, with the meaning of each word (*pl.* dictionaries)

Focus

a b c d e f g h i j k l m n o p q r s t u v w x y z

Remember, there are 26 letters in the alphabet.
Five of these are the **vowel letters**.
The other letters are called **consonants**.

Write the answers to these questions in your book.

1 What is the first vowel letter?

2 What is the last consonant?

3 What is the vowel letter following **h**?

4 What is the consonant after **o**?

5 What is the letter before **r**?

6 What is the middle vowel letter?

7 Which comes first, **m** or **n**?

8 Which comes first, **s** or **v**?

9 Which letter is between **k** and **m**?

10 Which letter is midway between **a** and **e**?

11 Is **p** nearer to **g** or **z**?

12 Is **n** nearer to **f** or **s**?

13 Which are the two vowel letters not found in the word **alphabetical**?

14 List the letters that are in the second half of the alphabet.

Remember, **alphabetical order** means the letters are put in the order of the alphabet.

The words in a dictionary are in alphabetical order.

Remember, if we are sorting words into alphabetical order and they begin with the same letter, we need to use the second letter in each word.

lace   lettuce   lime   lottery   lunar

(a) b c d (e) f g h (i) j k l m n (o) p q r s t (u) v w x y z

If the second letters are the same we need to look at the third letters.

shark   sheep   shield   shoal   shriek

(a) b c d (e) f g h (i) j k l m n (o) p q (r) s t **u** v w x y z

A Write these words in alphabetical order.
You will need to look at the second letters.

1 cud   cross   commit   chair
2 fine   feud   fable   flexible
3 mould   measles   magistrate   muffle

B Write these words in alphabetical order.
You will need to look at the third letters.

1 nurse   nudge   nut   number
2 fowl   four   forecast   fossil
3 curtain   cupboard   custody   cutlass

Extension

A Write your own short definition for each of these words. The first one is done to help you.

Remember, a **definition** is the meaning of a word.

1 luscious   sweet and delicious
2 explosive   3 automatic   4 efficient
5 atmosphere   6 crystal   7 impossible

B Use a dictionary to find the definitions of the words in **A**.
Copy them into your book.

Check-up 2

Focus

Write a word to match each picture.
Some letters are shown to give you a clue. Write the words in your book.

1 s_____g

2 fr_____

3 p_____

4 s_____

5 th_____

6 k_____

7 h_____

8 h_____

9 st_____

10 tele_____

11 _____f

12 _____t

13 f___n___

14 tr_____

15 _____l

16 t_____

17 _____t

18 s_____

19 f_____

20 e_____

Extra

A Write the plural of these words.

1 bell	2 bus	3 match	4 dress
5 box	6 dish	7 mystery	8 factory
9 play	10 library	11 monkey	12 fly

B Write the answers to these word sums.

1 walk + ing =	2 cry + ing =	3 slip + ing =
4 love + ing =	5 grumble + ed =	6 help + ful =
7 cry + ed =	8 happy + ly =	9 mercy + less =
10 please + sure =	11 slow + est =	12 merry + er =
13 smoke + y =	14 heavy + est =	15 shake + y =

C Add the prefix **un**, **dis**, **ir**, **in**, **im**, **il** or **mis** to these words to make them have the opposite meaning.

1 responsible	2 mature	3 patient
4 sure	5 legible	6 agree
7 visible	8 relevant	9 spell

D Add the prefix **de**, **re**, **pre** or **non** to these words to give them a different meaning.

1 sense	2 frost	3 fill
4 visit	5 view	6 stick

E Write contractions for each of these pairs of words.

1 he is	2 is not	3 he will	4 there has
5 I am	6 she would	7 do not	8 could not
9 does not	10 would not	11 should not	12 I would

Extension

A Write your friend's full name in your book. Write all the smaller words that you can find hidden in their name.

B Write the words in each of these groups in the order they would be in the dictionary.

1 chase   cluck   calf   costume
2 slippery   strong   ship   smoke   sudden
3 destroy   damp   dull   disappoint   donkey
4 apple   another   absent   adventure
   altogether   agree

C A silent letter has been left out of each of these words. Write the words correctly in your book.

1 com __   2 clim __   3 __ rong   4 __ ritten
5 __ nife   6 __ nock   7 d __ uble   8 c __ emist
9 s __ enery   10 ec __ o   11 sc __ ool   12 c __ aracter

D Choose the correct homophone for each of these sentences. Write each correct sentence in your book.

1 Are you enjoying this lovely whether/weather?
2 Have you scene/seen Dad anywhere?
3 The footballer mist/missed the goal!
4 Did you hear/here that noise?
5 Grip the reins/rains firmly.
6 We need flower/flour to make bread.

E Make an adjective ending in **ous** from each of these nouns.

1 danger   2 nerve   3 suspicion   4 victory